Because Life Goes On...

Helping Children and Youth
Live with
Separation and Divorce

A Guide for Parents

Healthy Canadians and communities
in a healthier world

Public Health Agency of Canada

Également disponible en français sous le titre
*Parce que la vie continue… Aider les enfants et les adolescents à vivre la
séparation et le divorce. Un guide à l'intention des parents*

For additional copies, please contact:
Publications
Public Health Agency of Canada
Postal locator 0904A
Ottawa, Ontario
K1A 0K9
Telephone: (613) 957-2991
Fax: (613) 941-5366

This publication is also available on the Internet at the following address:
http://www.mentalhealthpromotion.com

It can be made available on computer disquette or audiocassette, in large print
or braille on request.

Published by authority of the Minister of Health

© Her Majesty the Queen in Right of Canada, represented by the
Minister of Public Works and Government Services Canada, 2001

Reprint 1996, 2001, 2004
Cat. H39-293/1994E
ISBN 0-662-21513-3
Editions 1994, 2000

Acknowledgements

"Because Life Goes On... Helping Children and Youth Live with Separation and Divorce" is a Health Canada publication intended to reach out to Canadian families in need of information and resources to help their children to live through the process of separation and divorce. This booklet is also designed to assist professionals in such fields as social services, health, justice and education, in their work with children and their parents.

Health Canada is very proud to provide this 2nd edition of *"Because Life Goes On..."* in response to an overwhelming demand from Canadian families and professionals. Although the core content of the booklet has remained the same, certain sections have been updated to better address some of the current issues related to separation and divorce.

Health Canada is very grateful to all individuals who have contributed to the creation of this booklet, in particular to its authors:

Natacha Joubert, PhD, Mental Health Promotion Unit, Health Canada

Kathleen Guy, President of Guy Associates

Special thanks are due to those who provided their passion, commitment, and knowledge on the subject area or skills in research, writing, editing, translation and design. The Department expresses its appreciation to the following individuals and organizations for their assistance and collaboration, and to the many others, including our readers, who provided their ideas, suggestions and support:

BC Council for Families

Marilyn Bongaard, Karen Bron & Barbara Grocholski-Stewart,
    Child Support Team, Justice Canada

Joyce Borenstein, Illumination Magique Inc.

Michelle Décarie, Editor

Rhonda Freeman, Families in Transition, Family Service Association
    of Metropolitan Toronto

Liza Goulet, Consultant

Nancy Johnson, Johnson Associates

Orysia Z. Kostiuk, Parent Education, For the Sake of the Children Project, Province of Manitoba

Senator Landon Pearson, Senate of Canada

Stephanie Pelot and Lloyd Pelot, Pentafolio Multimedia

Marie-Josée Rosset, Translator

Suzanne Sabourin, Mental Health Promotion Unit

Annie Thibault, Cover Illustration

Gaby Vieira, Katalin Kennedy and Joanne Lacroix, Family Violence Prevention, Health Canada

Judith Whitehead, Vankellers Writing and Editing Services

Health Canada is also grateful to Justice Canada for their financial contribution to the printing of the booklet.

The quotations of young people included in this booklet are from the film video *One Divided By Two: Kids and Divorce.* Permission to reproduce these quotes was provided by the film's producer, Illumination Magique Inc. Refer to the Resources section for more information.

Table of Contents

V

Introduction

"HOW WILL THIS affect the kids?" is one of the first questions that goes through the mind of every parent facing the end of a relationship. The answers are as diverse as children themselves. Every child reacts to separation or divorce in his or her own way.

But even though every child is unique, there are needs and feelings that most children share. This booklet will help you understand those common reactions. With this knowledge, you will be better prepared to help your children cope, adapt and move forward.

We all know that divorce is tough on kids, both during and afterwards. But how you handle the separation and divorce can make a huge difference in how well your children adapt. Studies in child development and psychology show that children and youth adapt better if you:

- try to anticipate and understand your children's feelings, and do your best to help them feel safe, loved and secure
- help your children express their feelings — children of any age cope better when they feel they are being heard
- separate your spousal relationship (which has ended) from your role as parents (which goes on)
- protect your children from conflict between you and the other parent
- help your children keep a close relationship with both of you.

These are not easy tasks — especially during a time of emotional upheaval. But no one knows your child better than you do, and no one is in a better position to provide your child with security, routine, comfort and support. The love and safety you provide for your children during this stressful time will serve them for the rest of their lives.

There is no such thing as a perfect parent or an ideal family. Being a good parent doesn't mean having all the answers or solving every problem. It means demonstrating love and concern and helping children and youth understand and cope with their feelings. It means providing a safe and nurturing environment, and fostering a child's sense of trust and self-esteem.

Good parenting during separation and divorce is similar to parenting at other times. But just when children need extra attention and reassurance, your capacity may be reduced because of the stress of ending a spousal relationship. It's hard to "be there" for your kids when your own emotions are in turmoil.

The end of a spousal relationship is a very stressful and demanding time. Just as there are many times in life — such as the birth of a child or death of a parent — when some additional support or guidance can make all the difference, parents facing divorce will benefit from reaching out for the support and assistance they need.

All families, however, will benefit from taking advantage of community services and support networks. The "Resources" section will direct you to information and people who can help. If your family is dealing with violence, addiction or abandonment, locate professional guidance and support as soon as possible.

How This Booklet Is Organized

Because Life Goes On... is designed to provide parents and other adults with general information and suggestions. It also includes up-to-date resources and organizations available in your community and across Canada that can provide you with information, support and services.

Every family's experience with separation and divorce is different. There is no "typical" divorce and no "magic formula" for helping children deal with the process. The information in this booklet is not intended to fit every situation — some suggestions may apply and some may not. Use your judgement based on your family's unique situation.

The booklet is organized into six sections — each section builds on information contained before it, although you can easily jump to or read only those sections that meet your most immediate needs.

Section 1, *Parenting Through Separation and Divorce,* focuses on some of the challenges that you may face as you go through the process of separation and divorce, and how you can build a support network to help yourself manage better.

Section 2, *Helping Children at Every Age,* provides information on the stresses and challenges that children of all ages face during separation and divorce, and gives suggestions on how you can help your children adapt.

Section 3, *Parenting Is Forever: Developing a Cooperative Parenting Relationship,* outlines some of the key tasks for parents: to protect your children from adult conflict; to enable your children to have positive relationships with both parents; and to provide your children with nurturing, security and stability.

Section 4, *A Child's Age and Stage of Development Make a Difference,* is organized according to developmental stages — from infancy to adolescence. Although all children, pre-teens and adolescents share many of the same developmental goals and needs — such as a deep need to trust other people and their world — their particular age and stage of development are major factors in determining their reaction to any situation and how you can meet their needs.

Section 5, *Parenting After Separation and Divorce,* looks at some of the opportunities and challenges that children and their parents face as they go on with their lives. Old relationships change and new relationships develop. This section focuses on helping children adjust to two homes, to new parental relationships, and to remarriage and blended families.

Section 6, *Resources,* offers practical information on how and where to get support, assistance and information. No one should have to do it alone. Fortunately, there are resources available to help parents and children alike with their immediate and long-term needs. Whether you call a local agency, borrow a book from the library, or surf the Web, this section is designed to help you get the support you need.

Parenting Through Separation and Divorce

DIVORCE CAN BE such a painful experience that many parents find it difficult to respond to the needs of their children just when they need extra emotional support and attention. To help your children cope with divorce, you need to learn to manage your own feelings and new circumstances. This section focuses on some of the challenges that you may face as you go through the process of separation and divorce, and how you can build a support network to help yourself manage better. Like many other parents in similar circumstances, you can move on and help your children move on too.

Knowing What to Expect

Divorce is not a single event, but a process that unfolds over time. It involves a series of family changes and reorganizations that may take several years. The events and emotions that accompany these changes cannot be dealt with overnight. It takes time for everyone in the family to adapt.

Separation and divorce can be an emotional roller coaster. You may experience feelings of anger, isolation, anxiety, euphoria, depression, guilt, loss of control, fear, incompetence and insecurity. You may doubt your ability to deal with the needs of your children because you also face pressing needs of your own. Sometimes parents may feel that they have failed their children, and may doubt their own worth. These emotions and difficulties are a natural part of getting through separation and divorce.

New Challenges

There is no doubt that the process of separation and divorce is one of the most difficult experiences in an adult's life — socially, emotionally and financially. Most parents are ill-prepared for all of the challenges and adjustments they may face, including:

- Changing homes, neighbourhoods and schools, which may lead to a sense of instability and the loss of relationships and support systems.
- Economic changes — two households cost more to maintain than one. Some parents may face a sudden financial crisis. (See page 65 for information on how to get financial assistance.)
- Difficulty in concentrating on your job. Or you may immerse yourself in work, especially if you are no longer living with your children.
- If you are not living with your children, you may feel as if you've been cut off from their lives.
- You may have increased demands and responsibilities if you have the major role in caring for the children. It may seem that you don't have enough hours in the day to spend time with your children, and still find any time for yourself.

It's not surprising that with all the pressures of divorce, parents are under even greater stress. That's why it's so important for you to carve out some time to take care of your own needs. Try to schedule time for activities that help you get in touch with yourself, whether through a hobby, physical activity or simply relaxing quietly. Allowing yourself occasions to break away from the momentum of "doing" and simply "be", even for a few minutes, will help you regain your balance. It will give you a better sense of perspective and will help you stay on top of the day-to-day stress of work, children, and the separation or divorce.

Here are a few suggestions for activities to treat yourself to:
- take a walk
- photograph flowers
- enjoy a long soaky bath
- sing in a choir
- ...

Getting Help and Building a Support Network

All of us need "emotional" support as well as "practical" support. Family and friends, support groups, professionals, as well as other support services in your community, can all help you adjust to the changes in your life. It is important to reach out for advice, encouragement and understanding to help reduce tension and the feelings of isolation and depression that often go along with separation and divorce.

Also, by reaching out to other adults, you are teaching your children a very valuable lesson in life: we all need help from time to time, and learning from — and leaning on — others is an important part of living and growing.

Personal and Family Support

Most parents rely on outside support at one time or another.

- **Family and Friends** — Separated and divorced parents, especially those who live with their children, are often so busy with their child's day-to-day needs that they may neglect relationships with close family members and friends. Yet these people are the best allies you may have. They listen, give you a chance to enjoy the company of other adults, and help you get organized. They can become role models or sympathetic adults for your children. Family and friends can offer something crucial — compassion and understanding. Time alone with family and friends can help you get used to a new lifestyle.

- **Health Care Professionals** — Your family doctor, your children's paediatrician, or the staff at a community health centre are an important resource when you or your children are experiencing difficulties. They also can recommend other professionals or services available in the community.

- **Support Groups** — Many community centres and organizations offer support groups where people in the process of separation or divorce can talk about their feelings and experiences. Since parents often face similar problems, others in this situation can be a source of great comfort and inspiration.

- **Professional Counsellors** — If depression, anger or loneliness interfere with your work, home tasks or parenting, professional counselling from social workers, counsellors, psychologists or psychiatrists may help.

  If you are still considering ways to stay together, talking to an experienced marriage counsellor could be beneficial. A marriage counsellor can help you take steps to resolve conflicts, remedy past grievances and improve your relationship.

- **Family Mediators** — Family mediators can help parents resolve their disputes and develop a coparenting arrangement out of court. For more information on family mediation, see pages 27–28 and 66–67.

- **Community Resources** — There may be other resources in your community to help with your family's physical, emotional and social needs.

- **Family Service Agencies** provide a range of services, including family life counselling, educational programs, family violence prevention and intervention, and credit counselling and referrals.

- **Other Organizations and Services,** such as family- and youth-serving organizations, family resource programs, local religious congregations and community information and referral services can provide support, or help you find the help you need.

- **Local Libraries** have books, magazines, audio-visuals and Internet access on a range of helpful topics. Ask the librarian for assistance.

See pages 56 to 59 to locate these and other community resources.

Legal Support

The decisions that parents make during the process of separation and divorce are important and have long-term consequences. Family law is complicated, and everyone benefits from sound legal advice in this situation. There are a lot of family lawyers in Canada who can inform you of your rights and responsibilities. How much you must rely on your lawyer depends on your individual situation and on how you decide to approach it. See pages 67 to 69 for information on how to find a lawyer, apply for legal aid and obtain pamphlets about family law, the Federal Child Support Guidelines and other related issues.

Getting Immediate Help

If you are feeling "out of control," extremely depressed, or involved in child or spousal abuse, don't delay getting help. Some people or services to contact include:
- distress (help) lines (refer to the front page of your telephone book)
- hospital emergency departments
- shelters for abused women (phone numbers are often listed in the front pages of the telephone book)
- 911, police, fire or ambulance (refer to the front page of the phone book).

Helping Yourself Helps Your Children

Reaching out for support for your personal needs during separation and divorce will make you better able to respond to the needs of your children. Knowing more about how children, at each stage and age of development, experience separation and divorce will help too. The next section describes some of the feelings children and youth commonly experience as their parents divorce, and how you can help them adapt to the changes involved and move forward in their growth and development.

Section 2

Helping Children at Every Age

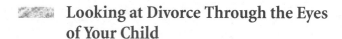 **Looking at Divorce Through the Eyes of Your Child**

Younger Children

It's important to keep in mind that however you as an adult understand or experience the situation, your children see and experience it differently.

No matter what their age, children have a limited ability to understand what is happening during a divorce, what they are feeling, and why. That doesn't stop them, however, from trying to figure out "the big picture." Younger children see things from their own perspective, that is, they see themselves as the cause of events. This is why younger children often blame themselves or invent imaginary reasons for their parents' separation and divorce. "If only I had behaved better or helped Mom and Dad get along better, they would still be together," many children say to themselves. They may imagine that their parents will walk out the door and never come back. Too afraid to tell anyone, they believe they are the only one in the world who feels this way.

Most children believe their parents will get back together, or wish that they would. Because of their limited ability to imagine the future, younger children cling to the only reality they know. Even children who have experienced or witnessed abuse may wish their parents would stay together. No matter what the circumstances, children develop a profound bond and a deep sense of loyalty to both parents.

Because children first learn and build their sense of self by watching and interacting with their parents, those children who witness parental arguing often experience it as though they are personally involved. Young children cannot separate themselves from their parents. Worse still, it is very hard for children to understand why the two most important people in their lives, on whom they depend for their very safety and survival, cannot get along. Just because they argued with a sibling or friend, that didn't make Mom or Dad leave. So why would Mom or Dad move out just because they have been arguing? Children do not understand why an argument would cause one of their parents to leave.

When parents continually argue, their children get caught in the middle. They worry about having to take sides and about pleasing both parents — a very heavy burden for a child.

Pre-teens and Teenagers

Children of this age have a growing ability to understand human problems. At the same time, they are becoming their own person. Developmentally, pre-teens and teenagers are going through a lot of change. They experience conflicting emotions and needs — sometimes torn between wanting independence and protection, freedom and guidance, love and detachment. Whereas younger children typically view divorce as the enemy, pre-teens and teenagers tend to hold their parents accountable for the divorce. They will most likely react to their parents' news of separation with anger, and older teenagers may wonder about their own capacity to build good relationships.

It's important to be aware that the emotional experience of anger is common to all children, just as it is to adults. But children, pre-teens and teenagers express it differently. As a basic human feeling, the experience of pain is at the heart of anger.

"They would fight a lot and I was really young, and I didn't really know what was happening and so I would think it was my fault. And I would sit in my room and not know what to do. And I always thought that maybe it was my fault."

LAUREN, 13

 ## Talking to Your Children About Your Separation and Divorce

Talking to your children about your separation and divorce is often the hardest and most emotional step in the process, yet how parents handle this crucial step can set the pattern for future discussions and influence the level of trust children feel in the future.

Telling your children that you are separating or getting a divorce will trigger a variety of responses that can vary from confusion, fear and sadness to anger, guilt and shock. Your children will want to know that you will not abandon them, physically and emotionally.

Take the time to handle this process thoughtfully and carefully. In particular, create a safe environment for these discussions with your children. For example, if there's too much conflict between parents, it's best for only one parent to explain what's going on. Here are some practical suggestions:

- Think in advance about a good time and place to talk to your children. Choose a place where your children will feel comfortable. It's a good idea to have subsequent conversations with each child alone, especially if there is a significant age difference between them. Their abilities to understand the situation and their reactions to the news are quite different.
- Keep in mind that most children would benefit from several shorter talks, rather than receiving all of the information at once.
- If appropriate to the situation, it's best for both of you to be together to tell your children. This will reassure them that they are not being abandoned and that you will cooperate in their future.
- Avoid waiting until the last moment. Contrary to popular belief, delay will not protect children from anxiety.
- Tell children, in general terms, why the separation is taking place. Remember to think about their age and stage of development. Children need to know that separation and divorce is not their fault. In other words, separation and divorce is an adult problem: "Mom and Dad could not find a way to work out our problems or to make things

any better. We've made mistakes and we're sorry that we're causing you pain."

- Plan what to say ahead of time. Above all else, be genuine. Depending on the circumstances, here are some messages that may be useful:
  - "Separation is a grown-up problem and you are not to blame. It is our problem and we will work it out."
  - "I/we know it seems unfair that these problems cause you pain and unhappiness. I/we wish things were different, too, but they're not, and we all have to work at accepting the changes in our family."
  - "We won't be living together any more, but we both love you no matter where either of us lives."
  - "You will always be part of a family."
  - "I/we want you to say what you feel and think. You may feel worried, angry and hurt. I/we understand because adults often have these same feelings too."

Give your children lots of opportunities to ask questions and share their thoughts and feelings. Because younger children may be afraid to ask questions or don't yet have enough experience to express their ideas, you may want to raise some questions that may be on their minds. If they are quiet during the discussion, remember that children need time to digest information. Be prepared to revisit the discussion and let them know that you are willing to talk about things as often as they need or want to.

Some children will have suspected a separation. For others, it will come as a complete shock. Children need time to adjust. Although some children may feel relieved that things are finally out in the open, they will still feel vulnerable and insecure. At first, children of all ages may not be able to imagine life without both parents under the same roof, no matter how strained or difficult family life may have been. Parents need to be patient with an unhappy child or youth.

Teenagers have the advantage of a growing maturity and understanding of human relationships. However, this greater understanding makes them aware of how life will change, from housing to disruptions in their school and social life. Therefore, pre-teens and teenagers will worry about how the divorce will affect them — both now and in the future. You can help by encouraging them to talk about their feelings, express disappointment and fears, and give them some say in how to deal with changes likely to occur.

You may be surprised by how much grief your children experience after hearing news of the separation. In some cases, a child's grief is quite profound. This can be very difficult and upsetting to deal with. Being a loving parent means that there are times when you may feel guilt. However, it's important not to let yourself think "I should have done more." As a parent, it's natural to always want to do the best for your children, but feelings of guilt are usually not in your best interests or those of your children. Guilt may add to an already deep sense of personal loss and sadness, and may provoke self-destructive thoughts. Feelings of guilt can also cause us to become defensive and closed to others.

Communicating Effectively with Children, Pre-teens and Teenagers

COMMUNICATING WITH your children is how you build their trust and sense of security, and assure them that their needs will be taken care of. These suggestions may help you communicate more effectively with your children.

Look for cues and clues. "Communication" is not the same thing for children as it is for adults. Children don't have the emotional and intellectual maturity to express themselves through words alone. Often, younger children communicate their innermost thoughts through playing, drawing, writing and building. By being attentive, you will learn to recognize and understand the meaning of your children's activities, facial expressions and body language.

Become a good listener. "Active listening" is a skill that you can learn to help communicate effectively — with adults and with your younger children. For example, by paraphrasing (gently repeating your child's statement in slightly different words), you can reassure children that they are being heard and understood. Active listening can also help children put a name to their feelings. As you are paraphrasing your child's statements, you can "label" the feelings the child is expressing, for example, "It sounds like you feel frustrated/you are angry/you are scared."

Build their understanding over time. Children can grasp more and more about a situation as they get older and develop more intellectual skills. Provide opportunities to go back to topics and talk about them again.

Give children and teenagers a say in their lives. You need to be in charge, not your children — but good parenting involves listening to your children and giving them appropriate choices so they don't always feel powerless. As much as possible, encourage your children to express their needs and opinions, and to be part of family decisions such as recreational activities, vacations, special occasions and clothes. Clearly, there is a big distinction between giving children choice in day-to-day activities, and putting them in a position where they are responsible for making adult decisions. But children need to know that their voice will be heard when adult decisions are made about issues that affect their lives.

Practice indirect communication with younger children. Indirect communication is a creative tool to help parents communicate with children. Many parents instinctively use indirect communication when explaining complex or confusing ideas to their children. You can use books, storytelling, hand puppets, dolls, action figures and drawings to help children talk about or act out their feelings. The type of indirect communication you choose will vary according to your own comfort level and your child's age and interests.

You can use indirect communication by telling your child a story about imaginary children in the same circumstances. The more these stories include the child's specific worries and fears, the more effective they will be. For example, you may tell the story of a child who feels sad because he can no longer kiss both Mommy and Daddy goodnight. By asking "how do you think the little boy in the story feels?" the child has the opportunity to talk about his or her own feelings. This technique is particularly effective for parents and children who have trouble expressing their feelings.

Indirect communication can help you to:
- give your children an opportunity to explore their feelings, without them worrying that you might be angry or disappointed
- help children realize that others face the same situations
- gain insight into your children's thoughts
- strengthen feelings of closeness and understanding between you and your children
- give your children some examples of healthy coping strategies.

Communicate directly with pre-teens and teenagers. Pre-teens and teenagers want to be respected for their growing maturity and viewpoints. When older children are spoken to as though they are young children, they are likely to feel insulted — just as you would. It is usually best to be direct with pre-teens and teenagers, and avoid giving lectures or disguising the point. But remember, you know your own children better than anyone. Use your judgement.

Pre-teens and teenagers want to have a say about the things they see as important. Although communication is not always easy with teenagers, you can provide opportunities for them to express their thoughts and feelings. Their developmental urge for independence and the need to be their own person create many opportunities for arguments. Some parents find it helpful to choose issues of disagreement very carefully. For example, what a teen chooses to wear to school is not an issue, but going to bed at reasonable time is not negotiable.

A direct style of communication, however, should not be confused with involving children in adult problems. Although your pre-teens or teenagers may even try to serve as your friend or counsellor, avoid placing them in those roles. Share your thoughts and feelings about the separation with other adults.

Maintaining Your Child's Community of Support

A child's community of support provides a place of belonging. This community includes family, daycare, school and friends — the people and places they come in contact with, and influence them almost every day in their young lives.

Grandparents and other members of the extended family are very important for children, especially if they have already established a close relationship. If they don't openly take the side of either parent, relatives can provide emotional security and be an important influence on children. Grandparents, aunts and uncles can help children by keeping in touch, spending time alone with them and assuring them that the divorce is not their fault. Pre-teens and teenagers, in particular, need regular contact with their friends, from talking on the telephone to spending time together at school and social activities.

Teachers and caregivers should be informed if there is a separation or a change of address. It is particularly important to let teachers and caregivers know who will be picking up the children and when, and who to call in case of a problem or emergency. Teachers and child care providers are especially significant since they spend so much time with your children. They can help provide a stable environment and a consistent routine. They can also help your children understand that they are not alone and that other children also experience separation and divorce. Good communication between teachers, caregivers and parents can help children adjust to the changes that divorce brings to their lives. They can play an important role by talking to you about any changes in your child's behaviour. Often, children do not express feelings directly, but teachers may notice signs of distress.

What Parents Can Do to Help Children at Any Age

- Children need to know how much they are loved by their parents. Be demonstrative — show your affection in words and actions.
- Create an environment where children are protected from conflict (for example, don't argue in front of them).
- Don't involve children in adult problems.
- Allow your child to express his or her feelings.
- Play with children. Play is literally the "work" of childhood. At all stages of development, playing alone, with adults and with friends helps children develop emotional, intellectual and social abilities.
- Avoid speaking of the other parent in negative terms.
- Spend some time alone with each child, even if it's just for a few minutes.
- Maintain as much routine and continuity as possible.
- Make sure children have opportunities to visit with relatives and spend time with friends.
- Stay in touch with child care providers and teachers. Most of

them will appreciate your input and involvement, and will be happy to share their insights and ideas. They are also good sources of information on child development and community resources.

- Set reasonable rules and limits for your children's behaviour according to their stage of development.
- If you make promises to your children, keep them.
- Take care of yourself. Your children are depending on you.

When to Get Help for Yourself and Your Child

Some situations require professional help. It is important for you, as a parent, to reach out for help when you are having trouble coping with additional demands, when you're dealing with violence or addictions, or when your child is in distress. Schools may have counsellors on staff or visiting psychologists or social workers. Parents and teachers should not hesitate to use them as a source of advice and information. For more information on where to obtain professional help, see the "Resources" section at the end of this booklet.

Violence in the Home

Separation and divorce can increase the likelihood of violence in the home, even in families where it has not occurred in the past. For women and children leaving an abusive home, the period after separation is often a time when the violence escalates. It is important for victims to find a safe place to stay and to develop a comprehensive plan to help them remain out of danger. A shelter for abused women can help you during this transition period.

For children and youth, violence in the family often has a traumatic effect, causing their behaviour to change. It is typical for them to be afraid, upset and angry. Even if they seem to be coping well, your children need extra attention and care.

"There's a lot of odd feelings. Feelings you never had before. Everyone says it's not your fault but you wonder sometimes."

ANDREW, 14

19

Regardless of their age, children from violent homes are at an increased risk of behavioural and developmental problems. They often suffer from anxiety and depression, and they may exhibit more aggressive, antisocial, inhibited or fearful behaviours. Even if they have not been assaulted themselves, children who are exposed to violence are emotionally abused. They experience similar symptoms to those children who are themselves physically abused.

Children who witness violence in the home often have a persistent fear for their own safety and the safety of brothers, sisters and the battered parent. They may also blame themselves for not being able to stop the violence (for example, by behaving better). For these children, feelings of self-blame, guilt, anger and fears about being different from other children may be more acute. They need help to understand that they did not cause the violence and could not have stopped it. They need to know that it is okay for them to feel angry and sad about losses that have resulted from the violence.

There are several things you can do to help your children deal with family violence:

- assure them that you love them;
- tell them as much as you can without name calling;
- listen to their feelings, assure them that these feelings are okay, and share some of your own feelings;
- don't be afraid to set limits in a firm, loving manner;
- take a little time every day to have some fun with them;
- encourage them to have friends and activities as soon as you resettle;
- let them be dependent — they need to be able to depend on you;
- be clear with them that no one deserves to be abused, and that violence of any kind is not acceptable; and
- let them know that you also have needs to have friends and to spend some time alone.

All parents should become familiar with signs of child abuse. Parents should seek help if their children have been abused or if they suspect abuse. Contact the local child welfare agency or seek advice at a family resource centre. Even if children have not themselves been assaulted, children exposed to violence in the family may need help. Counselling and support for you and your children can help all of you deal with this difficult situation. Refer to page 69 of the "Resources" section for specific information on where to get support and information.

Remember that you have made positive choices for you and your children. Credit yourself for your courage and strength.

A Child Who Experiences Abandonment

Abandonment can take many forms: the parent who walks away and refuses to have any further contact with the child, the absentee parent who rarely communicates with or sees the children only rarely, and the parent who slowly drifts out of the child's life over time.

Children who are abandoned by a parent may face significant problems. A child who is abandoned often feels an overwhelming sense of rejection. The thought that one parent no longer loves her, wants her, or even cares about her is potentially devastating to self-esteem and the future ability to form healthy, loving relationships. A child who has been abandoned may develop an intense yearning for the absent parent — a longing that can interfere with development.

Children who have been abandoned need to be assured that:
- they did nothing to cause the parent to leave
- they are very much loved and lovable
- adults sometimes have a hard time relating to others, and may do the wrong thing as a result.

Most children who have experienced abandonment by a parent will benefit from relationships with other adults who can serve as role models and provide them with experiences that would have been shared with the absent parent.

21

A Child in Distress

Children often react to stress by falling back on behaviours they have outgrown. But when this behaviour continues over time, or when your child is clearly not coping, it's time to get help.

There are some warning signs that a child is in trouble: anxiety, sadness and depression, eating or sleeping disorders, school problems, overly aggressive behaviour, alcohol or drug abuse, isolation from family and friends, and other unusual, persistent problems. It's always a good idea to seek help if you notice that a problem is persisting over time or getting worse. Some parents suspect sexual abuse when they notice their young children touching or stroking themselves. It's normal for young children to explore their bodies and comfort themselves by stroking their genitals. During times of stress, parents can expect that these natural behaviours may increase. However, if the behaviour persists or you are worried about it, you might want to discuss this with your family doctor.

If your child refuses to spend time with or see his other parent, this behaviour is telling you something important. Since children don't have the same tools as adults to deal with conflict and pain, they may react by shutting out one parent. Both the child and parent need each other to work through their feelings. Because a child's reluctance to interact with a parent may get worse and may interfere with his or her healthy emotional development, counselling is recommended.

For more detailed information, see "A Child's Age and Stage of Development Make a Difference." To locate community resources that can help you and your child, see the "Resources" section.

Parenting Is Forever: Developing a Cooperative Parenting Relationship

YOUR CHILDREN NEED both parents in their lives. But when your divorce is bitter, your continuing contact with the other parent can be very painful. That's one reason why parents need to rely on friends and other support networks to work through difficult feelings. Remember, too, that the passage of time can be a great healer.

Yet, however difficult it may be, working together as parents while you are separating as a couple is very, very important. When children are involved, your divorce ends the marriage, not the family. Your relationship as parents continues.

The key task for parents as your spousal relationship ends is to work toward building a cooperative parenting arrangement that:
- protects your children from adult conflict
- enables your children to have positive relationships with both parents
- provides your children with nurturing, security and stability.

Protecting Children from Parental Conflict

Most children are resilient and highly adaptive. With care and nurturing, they will adapt to separation and new family arrangements. However, when children witness a lot of ongoing parental conflict such as their parents shouting or threatening each other, their emotional development can be damaged.

"My parents never liked to talk directly with each other. My mother would tell me things to go tell my Dad, like for instance my Mom would say 'Samara, tell your Dad you need a new winter coat' and my Dad would say, 'Samara, tell your Mom that money's tight and maybe next week we can work something out'…"

"… Eventually I just

got very tired and fed

up with being this

messenger, and I said

'this has got to stop',

and 'I think it's about

time that both of you

start talking together

face to face or on the

phone'."

SAMARA, 13

Keeping adult conflicts away from children is one of the most important things you can do. In particular, using children as a way to punish the other parent is especially destructive for children of all ages. Parents who use children as a way to hurt the other parent use all sorts of damaging behaviours, such as blocking the other parent's access to the children, telling children about the other parent's shortcomings, or lying about the other parent's actions or intentions. Without exception, these tactics damage a child's health and well-being much more than the other parent.

Allowing Children to Have a Relationship with Both Parents

Children tend to do best after separation and divorce when both parents remain involved in their lives. Mothers and fathers are important to children for emotional support, protection, guidance, gender identity and their basic trust and confidence in themselves and in the world. Each parent plays a valuable role in child rearing. The task for children after the separation is to develop a separate relationship with each parent, and to spend time with each of them.

It is not uncommon for a mother or father to have such strong negative feelings about the other parent that she or he feels it is in the best interests of the children to prevent the other person from seeing them. Although this may seem like a natural protective response, it will likely harm your children's emotional growth and development. Of

THERE ARE UNIQUE ISSUES facing women and children who are emerging from an abusive or violent situation. Safety planning needs to be a central focus, above and beyond the development of a cooperative parenting relationship. Assessing the dangerous nature of the relationship is more important than encouraging parents to put the past behind them.

course, sometimes continuing the parent-child relationship is not advisable, or another type of relationship may be necessary (for example, when there is child abuse, spousal abuse or severe psychiatric illness). In those cases, a professional can help you make arrangements that are in the best interests of your children.

Building a Cooperative Parenting Relationship: Providing Your Children with Nurturing, Security and Stability

Working together as parents means sharing responsibility for your children's care and developing a way of making decisions that affect their health, education and welfare.

If you can't establish a civil relationship with the other parent, try to think of your relationship as having two parts. There is the marital part of the relationship which caused — and may still be causing — anger, grief and anguish. The other part is the parental relationship which will continue. It's in everyone's best interest to make it workable, but it's especially important for your children.

For a number of parents, it may be too difficult to talk directly with the other parent. This very understandable situation can be addressed by developing an "indirect parenting relationship." With this arrangement, parents communicate through letters, emails or another adult instead of talking with each other on the phone or in person. In addition, children can travel between homes with the assistance of another adult, or by being picked up by a parent at the child care centre or school.

The more you are able to achieve some kind of workable relationship, the better it will be for your children. Try to:
- respect each other's differences
- focus on the children, not on what the other parent may have done in the marriage or continues to do
- settle disagreements through give-and-take and compromise

- avoid making assumptions about the other parent's intentions or actions
- keep your agreements and promises (such as making child support payments on time, picking up and returning children on time).

The most important thing to keep in mind is that you are cooperating for your children's sake. Continue to keep conflict away from your children's ears and eyes. Over time, your relationship with the other parent may become easier and you may even develop a new understanding of each other.

How parents go about developing a parenting arrangement (or called "parenting plan") depends very much on their unique circumstances. In some families, the level of conflict is higher than in others. In these families, it may be difficult or even dangerous for parents to communicate directly. In other families, where the level of conflict is lower, it is possible for parents to sit down together and work out issues on their own. In most situations, regardless of the level of strife, conflict levels change over time.

One of the key ways to develop and maintain a good coparenting relationship is to make a written parenting plan. Agreed upon by both parents, a plan has a number of advantages and can help ensure that the children are well cared for by both parents. A written agreement that outlines specific arrangements and understanding of responsibilities helps reduce assumptions and misunderstandings. Also, a lot of planning and organization goes into moving children from one household to another. For example, your child may want to take his fish with him, or needs a clean uniform for a game the next day. Managing these kinds of details requires planning. If you're organized, it can reduce the chances of arguing with the other parent over little things. (The box on the following pages describes the role of family mediators, which includes helping parents develop a parenting plan).

Whatever situation you find yourself in, there are several options for resolving disputes. Refer to the "Resources" section to locate counsellors, family mediators, and family lawyers who can help you choose the best course of action based on your particular situation.

What Is Family Mediation?

FAMILY MEDIATION is a process to help parents resolve their problems and to develop coparenting agreements out of court. It gives you the power to make your own decisions and to settle your own differences. Mediation works if both parents are willing to compromise. Mediation can help you:

- separate your spousal role from your parental role
- focus on your children's needs
- concentrate on the present instead of the past
- explore various alternatives for resolving your differences
- reach an agreement on a parenting plan or other parenting issues.

Mediation may be a good option when both of you are determined to work toward a fair arrangement that protects the best interests of your children. It's not appropriate when there is violence, child abuse or neglect, chronic alcohol or drug abuse, or serious psychiatric illness on the part of one or both parents.

In mediation, a neutral professional helps you work out a plan on how to care for and share decisions about your children after separation or divorce. A solution agreed to by both of you is usually better than a solution imposed by an outsider such as a judge. Rather than pitting you against each other, mediation helps build the capacity of parents to work together on behalf of their children.

Mediation requires considerable effort. Negotiating with a former spouse in the midst of a crisis may seem impossible. However, the effort you put into the process can help reduce further conflict and ensure that the best interests of your children are kept as the focus of discussions.

THE MEDIATOR'S ROLE

The mediator may be a lawyer or mental health professional with specific training in family mediation. It is the mediator's role to help the family as it reorganizes, and to guide the decision-making process without taking sides or making decisions. Although the mediator must be skilled in family dynamics, child development, conflict management and the law, the mediator is not there to give legal advice, to write a contract or to provide therapy. The mediator helps you look at the pros and cons of the various alternatives in a cooperative way. The mediator does not pressure either of you into a particular position, but invites both of you to share what you are prepared to do.

THE MEDIATION PROCESS

The principles of mediation are the same whether dealing with parenting issues or financial matters, whether dividing parenting time or family assets. The mediator tells you about the divorce process and what decisions and issues you may face. He or she provides information and helps you understand your roles during and after the divorce.

INVOLVING CHILDREN IN MEDIATION

Children (usually over the age of 5) may be involved in some parts of the mediation process. The mediator may wish to:

- give children and teenagers an opportunity to talk about fears regarding their parents' divorce (this might include drawing pictures or writing a letter to their parents)
- gain an understanding of the children's developmental needs
- give children a chance to discuss their views about decisions affecting them.

See page 66 for information on how to find family mediation services in your area.

Section 4

A Child's Age and Stage of Development Make a Difference

ALTHOUGH ALL CHILDREN, pre-teens and teenagers share many of the same developmental goals and needs — such as a deep need to trust other people and their world — their particular age and stage of development are major factors in determining their reaction to any situation. Awareness of how children and teenagers grow and develop can help you predict how your children's behaviour may change and the kind of support they will need.

This section of the booklet is designed to help you:
- better understand the developmental needs and goals in each stage of your child's life
- anticipate and respond to your child's needs
- identify signs that your child may be feeling increased stress.

For each stage of development — from infancy to adolescence — you will find specific information about:
- divorce
- how children's development affects their feelings and reactions about separation and what you can do to help your children adapt and grow
- how to modify your parenting style as children grow up.

You may find it helpful to review the information contained under each stage of development, regardless of your children's ages. Reading the entire section may help you gain an understanding of how children change as they develop, helping you to anticipate your children's needs

29

and changing behaviours. Also, every child is unique: the way children react and the way you can respond may not "fit" their age categories precisely. Keep in mind that some feelings and needs occur during several stages of a child's development. And finally, remember that what works for one child at one stage may be equally helpful for another child at a different stage.

Infants and Toddlers (Birth–2 years)

There is incredible growth in children's development during the first two years of life. From birth, children quickly learn to understand a great deal of what is being said and happening around them. Physical development also proceeds rapidly, from crawling to running. Although these changes give children a sense of independence, they still rely almost totally on their parents. Infants and toddlers may become upset when the parent who takes care of them the most often leaves, if only to move into another room in the home. Being apart from this parent for just a few hours, even when the child is left with someone familiar, can be stressful.

During this critical stage of development, infants and toddlers need plenty of stimulation and loving attention. When babies receive warm, responsive care, they are more likely to feel safe and secure with the adults who take care of them. Very young children can sense the feelings of an upset parent and can become upset themselves. At any age, children are very vulnerable to the anxious and troubled feelings of their parents.

Despite rapid progress in learning to think, infants and toddlers still have a limited understanding of their world. Changes in routine and conflict between parents are bewildering and painful for very young children. Their lives can feel unpredictable, confusing and at times frightening after their parents separate.

Parental Conflict Is Harmful

Many parents don't realize how upsetting continued conflict with their former partner can be to infants and toddlers. You may assume that because very young children cannot understand the arguments they hear, they will be unaffected by them. In fact, although toddlers rarely understand the details of angry words between parents, they feel the emotions very strongly. It is important that you try to keep a calm, positive attitude in your child's presence.

Separation from Parents Is Difficult

Separation from a parent is difficult no matter what the circumstances. Attachment to a caregiver is key to an infant's healthy development. As long as there are no prolonged separations or serious threats to a baby's health, the baby will form an attachment to the main caregivers. Therefore, maintaining a strong bond with both parents is important for infants and toddlers. Frequent contact with the parent who no longer lives at home can help young children feel more secure. Parents who do not live with their children need to be patient with toddlers, giving them time to become reacquainted with each stay. Sometimes, the toddler's initial shyness is misinterpreted as a lack of love. The parent is under-standably hurt and discouraged and may see the toddler less and less, which makes the problem worse. More contact — not less — may help. It may also be helpful for the child to keep a photograph of the other parent. Both parents should do their best to help the toddler feel comfortable with parental visits.

Signs of Possible Trouble

Watch for signs that indicate a young child is experiencing difficulties — waking during the night, wetting the bed, not eating, aggressive behaviour, loss of language skills, loss of toilet training. (See page 34 for more information under "Reactions to Stress.") Infants and toddlers get angry when they are frustrated. Expect temper tantrums when schedules are disrupted, when enjoyable activities are cut short or are less frequent, and when they must wait to be fed, read to, cuddled or played with. Other indicators of distress include fearfulness and changes in mood, such as over-reaction to minor frustrations, withdrawal and listlessness.

Follow a Routine

Infants and toddlers need consistency and predictability in their daily life. Once parenting and child care arrangements have been made, it is up to the parent to maintain consistency in the child's schedule:

- the time of day the child is dropped off and picked up should be kept as regular as possible
- routines such as mealtimes, bedtimes and early morning rituals reinforce children's feelings of comfort and security
- try not to change a baby or toddler's personal environment (familiar surroundings, toys and blankets).

Preschoolers (3–5 years)

The preschool years bring rapid intellectual, physical and emotional growth. The developmental goal of a preschooler is to become independent.

Despite their considerable physical and emotional achievements, preschoolers have a limited ability to understand separation and divorce. For example, because they understand relationships in self-centred terms, children may feel that they are the cause of certain events. Children often believe that a parent's worries and anxieties, and perhaps even the divorce itself, are their fault.

Active Imaginations

Children between the ages of 3 and 5 also find it hard to tell the difference between what is real and what is imaginary. This means that they may become confused. Children may think that they are being abandoned by their mother, unloved by their father or that they are being

Pickering Public Library
Petticoat Creek
70 Kingston Road

Automated Phone Renewal
905-831-8209

Today's date: 10/22/2012 8:43:00 PM

3081008911209
The separation guide : know your opt
Due back on 11/12/2012

3081004391240
Helping your child survive divorce /
Due back on 11/12/2012

3081006926613
Divorce poison : protecting the pare
Due back on 11/12/2012

3081008063514
Because life goes on ... helping chi
Due back on 11/12/2012

Phone: 905-420-2254
www.picnet.org
Note: For security, client barcode
information has been removed.

punished for angry feelings. Preschool children are very curious and will actively try to understand the changes in their lives. They now have the ability to try to find answers themselves, and will ask "Why?" "How come?" and "What if?" This ability to understand some events may add to their worries.

Preschoolers are fond of listening to and creating their own "tall tales." They love to exaggerate stories, and they often believe the story they have just told. Parents should not confuse this with lying; in fact, you can use these stories as a way to exchange information and build better understanding. (See box "Communicating Effectively with Your Children, Pre-teens and Teenagers," page 14.)

The Need for Mother and Father

A preschool child's sense of social and emotional independence is not fully developed. Preschoolers continue to rely on their parents and a secure home base to feel safe. At this stage, children need nurturing from both parents — they are beginning to develop a relationship with their father that is different from the one with their mother. Children experience a significant loss when one parent is less involved in their lives. Not only will they often miss that parent's presence and affection, but some of their physical and emotional needs may not be met. They often have overwhelming fears that both parents will leave them. As with infants and toddlers, preschoolers need lots of visits with the parent who has moved away. Parents need to keep this in mind when they develop their parenting plan.

Personality Is a Major Factor

Personality is a major factor in development and plays an important role in a child's reaction to divorce. By the time children are 3 to 5 years of age, most parents can recognize the ways their children cope with stress. Some children sulk, others "talk back" or get angry, still others become overly submissive or obedient. It may be helpful to understand that when children are unable to express emotion and cope with stress in their usual ways, they try different approaches. Children who are usually outspoken or talkative may suddenly become withdrawn, and those who are usually submissive or obedient may suddenly become uncooperative.

Parents need to resist any temptation to let a submissive or obedient child become their caretaker or to ignore the child who makes fewer demands. It is also important to resist simply punishing an angry and disagreeable child instead of trying to deal with his or her underlying unhappiness.

Reactions to Stress

A young child's distress is often shown by returning to behaviours that have been outgrown. Problem areas may include:
- sleep — a return to bed wetting or recurrent bad dreams, avoiding going to bed
- eating — eating less or more than usual or refusing favourite foods
- physical activity — giving up drawing or riding a tricycle
- language — returning to baby talk
- emotional development — reverting to crying, clinging; or thumb sucking
- social relationships — refusing to play with other children.

Preschoolers can display a wide range of emotional behaviour in a short time. Anger is the most common way for preschoolers to show pain and distress. Hitting, kicking, throwing things, pinching and spitting at other children are common ways for young children to express anger. These expressions of anger toward friends or brothers and sisters often represent the child's disturbance or anger at the separation or divorce.

Fearfulness is also a sign of anxiety or tension in preschoolers, particularly when it is in response to events the child used to feel comfortable with. Troubled preschoolers may also show sadness, withdrawal or lack of energy.

Many of these feelings and responses in preschoolers can be related just to growing up. They do not, in themselves, indicate trouble.

However, if they are unusually intense, last a long time or interfere significantly with a child's life, they may be signs of distress.

Reducing Stress

You can help your preschooler adapt to separation and divorce by reducing the sources of your child's distress, and by providing reassurance, stability and comfort. Talking regularly about their feelings, fears and fantasies helps your children to work through their private, internal sources of distress. This requires you to listen closely to your preschoolers, observe their actions and respond by communicating with care and understanding.

Child Care Arrangements

Knowing with confidence who will take care of them, and where, provides preschoolers with feelings of stability and security. You can help by:
- selecting a regular setting for child care
- letting the child take familiar objects to the child care setting, such as stuffed animals, a prized blanket or toys
- maintaining a regular schedule for dropping off and picking up your child at the child care setting
- keeping consistent morning, dinnertime and bedtime routines.

If at all possible, it is helpful for you to keep your existing child care arrangements, at least during the beginning stages of separation and divorce. A familiar routine creates a feeling of security for children. When this schedule is disrupted, preschoolers may become upset. If changes in the daily schedule are unavoidable or necessary, you should explain the reasons for the changes. You can also help your preschoolers adjust by going with them to visit the new child care setting before they are dropped off for the first time.

Early Elementary School Children (6–8 years)

Although children of this age are forming outside friendships and attachments, the family is still the central influence in their lives. Like younger children, early elementary school children need time with both parents, or with role models of both genders. The relationship with the parent who no longer lives with them is very important to children at this age.

Early elementary school children are beginning to understand that parental conflicts are separate from themselves. Yet at the same time, they still base much of their self-image on how they and others perceive their parents. That's because children at this age are developing a keen sensitivity to what others might think about them or how they might judge them.

Use of Denial and Other Defences

Denial, in simple terms, means refusing to admit to yourself that you are hurting, or that anything is wrong. Denial is a typical reaction of younger elementary school children to separation and divorce. Children may also become angry and frustrated and bicker with brothers, sisters or classmates, or they may become stubborn and uncooperative at home. These are short-term attempts to cope with their own emotional pain, but neither denial nor anger is an effective defence in the long run. Denial prevents children from accepting and dealing with a difficult situation, while anger usually gets them into trouble with adults and peers at home and at school. Most importantly, neither of these defences helps children overcome their sadness.

Unexplained headaches and stomach aches can be the result of anger or anxiety. Fear and anxiety can also be shown in nervous habits, such as biting nails, rather than fear of a specific event or object.

Increased Capacity for Thinking

Children in early elementary school are learning to form complex thoughts. This results in the ability to imagine other future realities. For children whose parents divorce, this can mean that fantasies, such as being abandoned by the parent they live with, are more likely to arise. These fantasies worry children and heighten their distress over separation and divorce. If a parent remarries, children at this age may fear being replaced by a new baby.

A Strong Sense of Family

Early elementary school children have an increased understanding of their place in the family and how their family fits into society. As a result, their identity remains strongly tied to belonging to a family. Not only are their separate relationships with each parent important, but a love of and trust in their family have begun to emerge. Separation and divorce disturbs the feeling of family that is so important to children of this age.

Feelings of Loss

Deep feelings of loss and sadness are the primary features of the process of separation and divorce for young elementary school children. These feelings can come from:
- the loss of peace in the household because of parental conflict
- the loss of security when a parent becomes anxious or upset
- the change in or loss of a relationship with the parent who moves away
- a more distant relationship with the parent they live with because of increased work on the job and at home, or a new adult relationship or remarriage
- the loss of contact with grandparents and other extended family members
- the loss of a sense of stability, control over events and confidence
- the fear that their parents' divorce makes them different from their peers.

37

Prolonged Parental Hostility

As with children of all ages, strong or long-term hostilities between separating parents are a major source of stress for early elementary school children. Children at this stage of development are especially vulnerable to fantasies about what might happen when parents become angry, and they often worry that they may have caused their parents' marital troubles.

Early elementary school children want to help their distressed parent. Being needed by a parent makes them feel big, important and loved. Yet children also want their "same old" parent back, so that the parent can resume caring for "me." Children who are allowed to take on too much responsibility for taking care of their parents are robbed of many of the fun, carefree and spontaneous times that belong to childhood. They may develop into "little adults" who feel responsible and who cannot experience carefree times.

Communication Is Important

Parents can help early elementary school children adjust to the process of separation and divorce by talking clearly with them. Indirect communication may also help — stories about other children who have gone through divorce can help your child see how some other children cope and help her realize that she is not alone. (See page 14 for more information.)

Tell your children the reasons for the divorce, using an approach and language that's appropriate to their age. Sometimes, it may not be wise to tell them the specific reasons and the details. (See page 12 for some examples of how to talk with your children about divorce.) Assure them over and over again that the divorce is not their fault.

Many parents hesitate to have the first talk with their children because they don't want to hurt them. However, some pain is unavoidable. Children may already be sad and upset by their parents' arguing and by a general feeling of stress and tension. They may feel relieved by finding out what is really going on, and what is going to happen to them.

The first talk is an opportunity for you to take responsibility for the problems. It allows your child to know what to expect, and to feel relieved that the arguments may come to an end.

Children need to know exactly what will happen to them. The more information you can give them, the better. Children want to know:
- where they will live and with whom — whether the home is changing or not, they need reassurance of where home will be
- how often and where they will see the other parent — including the kinds of activities they may do together and what the limitations are, if any
- any changes to the family's schedule or routine, such as a parent returning to work or new chores
- how their sisters and brothers will be affected — for example, will all of the children spend time together with the other parent, or just separately?

If a change of school is unavoidable, give your children every opportunity to learn about the new school before they start. Also, if one of you is planning a major move, give your children as much time as possible to handle this change in their lives.

Encouraging Discussion

It is particularly important for early elementary school children to have opportunities to talk about their feelings and ask questions about the divorce and what will happen to their family. As hurt and upset as you may be, it is important to put aside this pain when you talk to your children. Assure them that most children have all sorts of feelings when their parents divorce, and that these feelings are okay.

Asking for Help

Ask teachers and other caregivers to watch for changes in the actions and attitudes of your child. The more you know about your child during this transition, the better able you are to help him or her adjust.

Pre-teens (9–12 years)

Significant social and emotional growth gives pre-teens an increasing sense of independence. This feeling of independence means they place greater importance on the world outside their family. They have greater involvement in school, friendships and extra-curricular activities.

Pre-teens have a growing understanding of human relationships and a realistic understanding of divorce. But although they understand more, they are still not able to deal emotionally with everything they experience. During this period, children are forming an internal code of moral values, largely based on what they learn from parents and other adults.

Social Withdrawal

Social withdrawal is a common sign of worry or fear among pre-teens. Relationships with other children and friends are crucial to the social and emotional growth of children at this age. Lack of involvement in activities with other children outside school or a change in social groups may be a signal to parents that a child is troubled.

Helplessness Turns into Anger

Pre-teens will frequently convert feelings of helplessness and sadness into anger. Anger helps prevent them from feeling unhappy and emotionally vulnerable — it's a way of dealing with their pain. Some pre-teens may show aggression, either directly through physical fighting with schoolmates and brothers and sisters, or in bitter, verbal attacks directed at one or both parents. Or a child may argue heatedly with you or complain about curfews, television rules and having to do household chores. Your pre-teen's conflicts may also be expressed as physical problems — headaches or stomach aches that are very real and painful.

A Need to Please

Pre-teens may also try to cope by maintaining good relationships with both parents at all costs. They may try to gain praise and attention by being overly attentive and helpful to one or both parents and at school. By showing so much self-control and sympathy, they often sacrifice their own needs, assertiveness and strength of character.

Developmental Needs Neglected

Although children of this age long to be treated like adults, parents need to resist the temptation to involve them in adult problems. For example, letting them choose the colour of paint for their room is far different from involving them in financial affairs. While many children are willing to provide support to their parents, they are too young to take on this kind of responsibility. Be aware that children who grow up "taking care of their parents" run the risk of emotional difficulties later in life. To make sure your children's developmental needs are being met at this age, encourage them to make friends and to take part in activities outside the family.

Emotional Costs of Conflict

As with children of any age, the emotional costs of allowing pre-teens to become directly involved in adult conflicts can be considerable and long lasting. Pre-teens experience conflicting loyalties. They may experience strong feelings of guilt, disloyalty and fear. When parents draw children into the conflict, it places children in the unbearable position of choosing one parent over the other. Children of this age are not ready to handle this power or cope with the stress it creates.

New Adult Relationships

When a parent begins to see someone new, pre-teens must deal with the reality that the parent will have less time and energy for them. They may:

41

- confuse having less of their parent's time with having less of their parent's love
- consider their parents "still married"
- not be ready to recognize their parent's sexuality — they have difficulty imagining their parents in a sexual relationship
- feel conflict about whether they should enjoy being with their parent's new partner.

A Wide Variety of Defences

Pre-teens use more elaborate defences than younger children. For example, they may show their fears in ways that do not make them appear vulnerable or in need of help. It may seem that they are upset at someone else — another child, family member or teacher — or are not experiencing trouble or anger. Depending on the maturity level of your child, it may — or may not — be helpful for you to confront these defences directly. For example, some 9 year olds think and act like they are going on 15 years of age, while others seem to act their age. Use your judgment based on how your pre-teen has responded in the past. If direct communication about their defences or feelings might be interpreted as threatening or invasive, you may want to approach the topic through indirect communication, such as talking about the feelings of characters in a movie. (See page 14 for more information on communicating with your child.) Some defences pre-teens may use are:

- denying feelings, such as discussing upsetting events in an unemotional way
- displacing feelings, such as fighting with friends and other children instead of showing anger at a parent
- becoming overly devoted to a parent
- idealizing and identifying with the absent parent.

Pre-teens Need Reassurance and Support

Parents sometimes think it's not necessary to explain divorce to their pre-teens because they are mature enough to see for themselves what is happening. Despite the apparent "sophistication" of some children this age, it isn't true.

Children naturally turn to their parents for understanding, reassurance and support in difficult times. When you do not discuss your separation and divorce, children are cut off from their basic way of coping with their questions, worries and troublesome feelings. You can explain the separation and divorce to your pre-teens in a manner which reflects their level of maturity. Some pre-teens are young for their age and might relate better to communication styles appropriate for younger elementary school children, while other pre-teens might respond best to a direct approach that is best suited for teenagers (see page 14).

Pre-teens need you to show your commitment in concrete ways. When you make time to attend school meetings, performances and athletic events, it shows your children that you are there for them. You can help your children build confidence and self-esteem — encourage them to develop their interests in school, sports and arts, help them make new friends, and acknowledge their new-found strengths and growing maturity.

Parents should continue to enforce reasonable limits, rules and curfews — pre-teens need structure and routine to feel secure. Relaxing the rules to compensate for feelings of guilt over the separation and divorce often leads to further problems.

Other adults can serve as allies and role models for your pre-teens. Find opportunities for your children to spend time with other trusted adults, such as relatives, neighbours or teachers.

Teenagers (13–17 years)

During adolescence, teenagers are learning to define who they are and to develop their own values, priorities and goals. Teenagers are also gaining a sense of belonging to a community and to the world around them. In short, teenagers are developing their own identity, a unique identity that is separate from that of their parents.

It's tough being a teenager, even under the best of circumstances. Teenagers have lots of questions, and you may not have all the answers. The teenage years are a time of great change, which adds to confusion and stress. Emotionally, teenagers try to adapt to physical and social changes while trying to become more independent from their parents. More than ever, teenagers need emotional support, love and firm guidance from their parents as they confront these considerable challenges. Despite their physical maturity (and claims for independence) teenagers still need their parents.

Most teenagers see their parents as having positive qualities as well as limitations and faults. After separation or divorce, teenagers may begin to see their parents only in negative terms. Teenagers often have difficulty understanding how their parents could have let their relationship deteriorate. They may begin to perceive their parents as selfish, stupid, weak or cruel. These impressions are often strengthened as children watch their parents fight or grieve.

Conflicting Emotions

Because of the confusion and turmoil of the teenage years, stability in their lives is important. This is why parents' separation or divorce is one of the most difficult life events for a teenager. However, compared to younger children, they have greater resources to help them handle those challenges.

When parents divorce, teenagers experience two sets of changes: those that happen before the separation and divorce, and those that occur during the process itself. They are often genuinely shocked to learn that their parents are separating. Although they usually have been aware of tension between their parents, most teenagers do not believe that they will actually divorce. Surprise and shock are quickly followed by anger and sadness. Teenagers do not like having their lives disrupted. And they are often disappointed because their parents could not keep the family together. Teenagers often recognize their own feelings, but rarely understand exactly why they are angry, sad or intensely critical of their parents.

Teenagers may feel some of these common conflicts:

- anger at one parent or both parents, versus love for both parents
- loyalty to both parents, versus the tendency to take sides or choose one parent over the other
- affection for a parent's new partner, versus anxiety over sexuality in the parent's adult relationship
- giving the appearance that everything is fine, versus the need to be cared for and protected.

Teenagers experience other difficulties as well. They may see the separation as "proof" that the parent who leaves does not really love them or want to be with them. Teenagers are also vulnerable because their parents may try to use them as spies and messengers, but they may also strongly reject this role as well.

Anger: A Common and Visible Emotion

Teenagers are sometimes overwhelmed by their own anger. Intense conflicts between parents can be very upsetting to them. They find it difficult to admit that their parents put themselves in such unpleasant circumstances and that they hurt each other so much. Teenagers may also learn from arguing parents that the uncontrolled expression of anger is acceptable (or the opposite — that anger should be concealed or disguised). Troubled teenagers often express anger toward parents, brothers and sisters, teachers, friends, other children and physical objects. Fighting, destruction of property, and yelling and screaming are the clearest examples of anger in action. Drug and alcohol abuse, withdrawal or refusal to participate in activities, poor grades, skipping school, stealing and poor eating habits are often the result of anger, although the teenager may not be aware that anger is motivating this behaviour.

"… At first I didn't know how to get angry. I didn't know if I should just talk about it or if I should scream. Because I never really talked about the divorce with my friends. I just never thought that anybody would really understand."

MELISSA, 17

A child's age
can make a
difference

Other Common Responses

In addition to anger, teenagers may also:
- feel a great amount of stress
- develop a fear of the future
- feel an exaggerated need to organize their world
- question the concept of marriage and whether it can last
- worry if they will ever be able to have happy relationships themselves
- perceive parental dating as a threat or resist a parent's new partner.

Direct Communication Is Best

Although younger children often benefit from indirect communication, teenagers can cope with the news better if both parents discuss the separation and divorce directly with them. It is best for you to talk with teenagers together with any younger children in the family, and then again separately. This helps teenagers feel that their increasing maturity is recognized.

Parents should talk realistically about the divorce and what they think it will mean to the everyday life of their teenagers. Parents can stress the need for mutual patience and sensitivity; just as it takes time for teenagers to adapt, parents don't "have it all worked out" either.

Direct communication and a willingness to compromise on some issues of disagreement will help teenagers adapt to their new circumstances and continue the regular growth and development of adolescence. A sensitive balance of direct communication, negotiation which acknowledges their needs while setting reasonable limits, and respect for their growing independence will be most effective.

Help Teenagers Keep Their Friends

It usually helps to keep teenagers in their current school where they have already developed a network of friends. Some of these friends may have experienced divorce in their own family. Make sure that teenagers see their friends regularly, and that the separation and divorce process does not take up all of their time and energy. It's natural for teenagers,

regardless of whether their parents are together or separated, to sometimes choose to spend time with friends or extended family members
rather than with a parent. If there is a move to a new location or long
trips between their parents' residences, teenagers will need to make new
friends and adapt to new situations, which can make this life event even
more difficult and stressful. It will take time for them to adjust.

Parenting After Separation and Divorce

AS SEPARATION AND DIVORCE is a process that can go on for several years, the period following a formal separation involves many life changes and decisions — and all of them have an impact on younger and older children. Fortunately, there are many good books and resources for parents and young people on topics such as dating after divorce and remarriage, blended families and step-parenting. The following section highlights some of the key issues involved with parenting after separation and divorce. For those parents who would like to explore these issues in greater depth, please refer to the "Resources" section for some suggested books and pamphlets.

Helping Children Adjust to Two Homes

Children of any age do not like to have their security threatened. Their security comes from a sense of predictability and a stable family environment. Children's sense of security is often built around the familiarity of where they live, eat, sleep and keep their possessions. This sense of "home" takes time to rebuild when they begin moving between residences.

When children begin the process of travelling between two homes, they experience feelings of loss, confusion, anxiety and insecurity as they adjust to the reality of being with one parent at a time. As a coping mechanism for trying to handle these emotions, they may over-react and become very difficult to handle for a few hours or even days. One parent may blame the other for this behaviour, assuming that the other parent is not disciplining the child, or is even encouraging the child to behave badly. But it's important for you not to jump to conclusions — your child's behaviour may be nothing more than a reaction to his or her own feelings of grief and loss.

When children move between homes, they are constantly reminded that the family is no longer together. Children may also experience separation anxiety from one or both parents, or they may worry about the well-being of the parent they are leaving behind. In addition to all that, children have to deal with some unwelcome changes in their schedule and environment. Give children time to adjust to the changes, and make sure they feel safe and secure in both places. For example, you can work together to ensure that your children have familiar belongings and favourite games with them at each residence. You can also help children maintain visits with friends and extended family members.

If one parent moves a great distance away, a child's feelings of loss and anxiety may be understandably heightened. In the case where one parent sees the children during holidays and summer vacations, it's important to help maintain continuity as much as possible by keeping the residence "homey" and filled with some familiar possessions. Parents also need to prepare their children for the inevitable changes and how they will maintain contact with both parents. For example, regular phone calls can help children maintain a continuous relationship with a parent who lives at a distance.

"I do miss my Dad because he lives far away and I only see him five times a year. I wish that I could live in the same city as him — that way I could see him and my family…"

When You Live Apart from Your Children

IF YOU DON'T LIVE with your children, it's sometimes easy to believe that you are not needed any more. But children need and want both of their parents in their lives. Children who have lost touch with one parent often feel a longing for that parent that

49

"… And sometimes

we could bond, like

two men together. We

could go camping in

the wilderness, we

could play pool, he

could teach me how

to shave, how to

drive a car, and we

could talk about girl

problems."

TERRY, 13

never goes away. Just knowing that his parent loves him, and is still acting as a parent, has a profound effect on a child's well-being and sense of self-esteem. You cannot be replaced.

- It's important to be consistent and reliable. Your children count on you to do what you say you will do. Discipline should be consistent – don't ignore discipline and don't over-do it. Enjoy your time with your kids.
- As your child grows, so will your relationship with her. Young children need to be with you more frequently. Teenagers will want more time with their own friends.
- Invite your child to bring a friend along on a planned activity. Take lots of pictures and give your child a set of prints.
- Encourage your child to bring special things to show you (like a school project, badges, special reports or photos.) Give him his own bag to use when bringing these possessions.
- Celebrate holidays and birthdays around the actual date. Try creating some new holiday traditions.
- Send your child letters, postcards or email. Stay in touch. All these reminders show children how much you love them.

Remember that you are building a relationship with your child that will last forever.

When Parents Start Dating

In some families, a new adult relationship may have started before the separation, or may begin in the early stages of separation and divorce. In others, a new person may not enter the picture for months or years. Many single parents are trying to keep up with the extra demands of parenting on their own, and have little time or energy to spend on developing a new relationship. Some parents don't want to start going out with someone new — they may feel insecure about where to meet others and how to approach them, uncertain about their attractiveness, and concerned that they might fail in another relationship. For others, dating helps them adjust to divorce. It reaffirms their self-worth, reduces feelings of loneliness, and helps them get on with their lives.

Whatever the circumstances, dating may trigger emotions that are similar for both parents and children. They may be fearful of being hurt again, worry that they may not be loved by the new person, and have concerns about how the new person will fit into their lives. Parents can use this new situation as an opportunity to talk about how adults — just like children — need peer interaction with people their own age, and supportive relationships.

If the marriage ends after one parent leaves the relationship for another partner, children may feel particularly betrayed and angry. Children in these families will need plenty of opportunities to express their confusion and feelings — a difficult task for a parent who may be experiencing similar emotions.

Children have mixed emotions about their parents' new relationships. Depending upon their age, they may feel betrayal, jealousy, anger, confusion and even guilt. For example, they may feel:

- that the parent who is first to begin a new relationship is betraying the other parent. The parent can explain that people adjust differently, and that it is time for him or her to meet and go out with new people, even though the other parent may not be ready to begin another relationship.
- the parent-child relationship doesn't give parents the opportunity to do all the activities that adults like to do. It's important to keep on reminding children that friends and new partners do not replace the love between a parent and a child.
- their parents may get back together again. No matter how often parents have told children that getting back together won't happen, many children continue to hope, even after a second marriage.
- embarrassed that parents have sexual feelings and a need for affection. This is especially true for children in their pre-teens and early teens. Parents should explain that they, like other human beings, have sexual feelings and that these are a natural part of adult life.

- they have been abandoned again and experience a renewed loss when parents spend time with another adult. Finding extra time for the child while seeing a new person is difficult, but important.
- anger at being forced by adults to make another adjustment. How children act out this anger depends on their developmental stage. Clear and sensitive communication is the key to helping children cope with the adjustment.
- anger that parents have their own rules for sexual behaviour and enforce what may seem like different rules for their children. Teenagers are especially likely to feel that while they have curfews or have to date people their parents know and approve of, their parents seem to follow a different standard. Explain that there are two sets of rules — one for adults and one for teenagers — and explain why this is so.
- anger at the loss of privacy. Children need space they can call their own. It is important that new partners respect that space and treat children as individuals in their own right.

Sexual Orientation and Divorce

WHEN ONE OF THE DIVORCING PARENTS is gay or lesbian, it adds additional dimensions to the situation. If both parents are comfortable discussing issues related to sexual orientation — if both are able to answer their children's questions simply, without going beyond what the child is asking for — children usually will be more comfortable with the knowledge that one of their parents is gay. The important thing is that children are reassured that both parents will continue to love them, despite the situation they are living in.

However, children of a gay or lesbian parent may be teased and deeply hurt by their schoolmates. Homosexual parents may also face discrimination from families, co-workers and the community which can be difficult to deal with. This can be especially true once new parenting arrangements are made.

Children, particularly teenagers, may feel confused about their own sexuality and personal identity. They need an open atmosphere at home in which to ask questions and share their concerns or fears. If children or parents find the topic difficult to discuss, a knowledgeable counsellor may be able to help.

Changes will be easiest for children if parents can work out the issues in their own relationship without involving the children. Self-help groups may also be available in the community to provide support to parents dealing with issues of sexual orientation and parenting. Groups for children of gay or lesbian parents may also be available.

Remarriage and Blended Families

Remarriage is one of the most common challenges facing children whose parents divorce. Children who have not adjusted to parental dating will have even more intense problems as they try to adjust to their newly blended family. Remarriage leaves no hope of the parents getting back together, although some children continue to fantasize about everybody living in one home again.

Children may also have to deal with step-brothers and step-sisters, new grandparents, aunts and uncles. They may find it hard to accept changes in discipline and the authority of the step-parent. They may be jealous of the time and attention given to the new partner, step-brothers and sisters. They may feel that they are treated unfairly compared to their new siblings. A new baby may also spark feelings of anger and insecurity. Parents may find that being aware of these issues can be useful as they help their children adjust to new situations.

Step-family relationships or "blended families" differ from original family relationships in many ways. When families are reorganized, children often experience having more than one "mother" or "father." Most children adapt to this. Parents who have formed new relationships should make a special effort to spend time alone with their children. They need to know that they are part of the new life you are building.

The step-parent enters a new family group that already has a shared history, strong bonds and an established way of operating. Acknowledge that you will never replace their mother or father, and work on developing a unique relationship with the children. Encourage your step-children to honour and respect both of their parents and not to take sides. A step-parent can be a special friend to the children. Try not to compete with, replace or be critical of the other parent. When step-parents criticize the children's parent, children feel worse about themselves and less loving toward the step-parent.

In many cases, step-parent and step-children are suddenly thrown together, without the chance to develop a relationship gradually. The clashing of different rules, goals, definitions of behaviour and methods of child rearing can cause many problems, and a satisfying relationship between step-parents and children usually develops slowly. This is not surprising, since closeness, affection, friendship and trust usually need time to develop.

Step-parents can help children deal with changing roles and circumstances by being patient and giving them lots of time to adapt to their personality and lifestyle.

Many good books and articles have been written about remarriage, step-parenting and blended families. See page 74 for some authors and titles.

Because Life Goes On...

The challenge of being a parent during separation and divorce may sometimes seem overwhelming. When times are hard, it is important for parents to remember that all children face challenges as they grow up. Some move from school to school, from community to community. Some experience the death of a family member — a grandparent or older relative, and sometimes a parent or sibling. Some face serious illness. And through it all, they cope and learn and mature. Children have a tremendous capacity to meet the challenges life throws them. They have a remarkable ability to bounce back from difficult experiences — and this ability grows out of being loved and cared for.

Use your good judgement and common sense, try some of the suggestions outlined in this booklet, and reach out for the support and assistance you need from friends, family, professionals and community resources.

Despite the difficulties and pain, separation and divorce — like other challenges in life — can provide opportunities for growth, for both parents and children. Just as you may gain confidence, acquire new strengths and develop new abilities at this time in your life, so will your children. By helping them deal with divorce, you are giving them the skills to manage other challenges in life.

Because life goes on…
Because we are called to respond to its challenges…
Because we best see the light with our eyes wide open.

Section 6

Resources

How Can I Locate Information and Resources?

Making Use of Community Organizations

Refer to the Yellow Pages of your phone book for a listing of community organizations by looking under a heading such as "Social Service Organizations." Many cities and towns have community information centres with trained staff or volunteers. They can give you free information about services in your area.

Depending on the size and location of your community or city, the following organizations may exist in your area. Their programs and resources are there for your benefit.

Family Service Organizations

Over 120 family service organizations in Canada provide programs and services such as family life counselling, educational programs, family violence prevention and intervention, debt management and referrals.

To find the family service organization in your area, refer to the Yellow Pages of the phone book under a heading such as "Social Service Organizations." Look for the name of an organization (or organizations) with a title such as "Family Services," "Family Service Bureau," "Family Service Centre," "Family and Children's Services." Sometimes the name of these organizations is preceded by the name of your town, city or province, or by a religious affiliation such as "Catholic," "Protestant" or "Jewish."

Family Service Canada is a national non-profit organization representing family-serving agencies across the country. For assistance in locating an agency in your area call 1-800-668-7808, or contact them at:

Family Service Canada
383 Parkdale Avenue, Suite 404
Ottawa ON K1P 5Z9
1-800-668-7808 or (613) 722-9006
Fax: (613) 722-8610
Email: fsc@igs.net
http://www.cfc-efc.ca/fsc/

Their website lists resources designed to assist people in their relationships, in critical times and in day-to-day living. Services are directed toward parents, children, youth, service providers and community leaders. For example, topics on their website include:

- *Helpful Hints for Healthy Parenting*
- *Coping with Tricky Times*
- *Promoting Your Child's Self-Esteem*
- *Supportive Ideas for Raising your Child in Separate Homes*
- *When Parents Separate or Divorce: Helping Your Child Cope*
- *Self-Help Groups and Support Groups for Parents and Children*

Canadian Mental Health Association

Over 140 branches of the Canadian Mental Health Association (CMHA) are located in communities across Canada. In addition to community services and programs, CMHA distributes inexpensive pamphlets on parenting, separation and divorce, including:

- *Separation and Divorce*
- *Children and Depression*
- *Children and Difficult Behaviour*
- *Children and Family Break-up*
- *Children and Self-Esteem*
- *Children and Their Fears*
- *Children and the Stress of Parenting*

To locate the CMH... ... in the ... ...
the Canadian Ment... ...

> Canadian Me...
> 2160 Yonge St...
> Toronto ON ...
> Tel.: (416) 484...
> Fax: (416) 484...
> Email: cmhan...
> http://www.cm...

For pamphlets, conta... ...
form provided, or cal... ...

Other Community Organizations

Other organizations may offer services and programs for you and your children, such as information and referral agencies, family resource programs, United Way/Centraide, Friendship Centres, YMCA and YWCA. Refer to your phone book for these and other organizations available in your community.

Using the Internet: How to Gain Access to the Information Highway

THE INTERNET IS A NETWORK of networks, linking computers to computers. It is sometimes compared to a giant international plumbing system. The Internet itself does not contain information; rather it finds documents found on computers linked to the Internet.

Industry Canada supports various initiatives designed to help provide Canadians with affordable public access to the Internet and the skills to use it effectively. These initiatives include the Community Access Program, SchoolNet and

LibraryNet. For those readers who would like to learn more about the Internet and how to gain access to it, the best place to start is by calling your local library. Many libraries are set up to help you learn about this tool and to use their specially designated computer terminals. If your library does not have these services, it may be able to connect you with organizations in your city or community that do.

This Resource section lists a large number of websites that contain information on topics related to helping children through the process of separation and divorce. The beauty of the Internet is that all of this information is at your fingertips. The disadvantage of the Internet is that, although you can find a wealth of information on almost any topic, the quality or accuracy of the information varies widely. That's why it's important to know a bit about the reliability of the source of the information you have located.

If you're just getting started on the Internet, there is one website that we suggest you begin with: The Canadian Child Care Federation's website called "Child and Family Canada," supported by Human Resources Development Canada and Industry Canada (http://www.cfc-efc.ca/cccf), contains a wealth of useful information provided by over 45 collaborating voluntary organizations. This website includes information and resources on topics such as child care; family resource programs; child development; family life; health; learning activities; literacy; media influences; parenting; physical activities and play; child safety; social issues; special needs; and adolescent health and well-being.

For a listing of other websites on parenting and family life, and of websites designed specifically for children and youth, refer to the Public Health Agency of Canada's Mental Health Promotion Unit website (see box on page 63).

Making Use of Municipal Services

Various government programs and services are also available to serve children and families at the local level. A community organization or your family doctor can provide information about them, or they can be found in the phone book's Blue Pages under:

• Municipal Government — Headings such as community centres, health information, social assistance, child care information, children's services and health, employment, and information and referral centres.

Accessing Provincial Services and Organizations

Your provincial government is responsible for providing health and social services throughout the province, including health care, family and children's services, courts of law and legal aid.

• Refer to provincial listings in the Blue Pages under general information, children's services, community and/or social services, courts (family court, mediation services, legal aid services), family benefits, and housing.

• Provincial and territorial departments of Justice (Family Law Division), Social Services and Health usually have resources available (i.e. free pamphlets, brochures). You can access provincial and territorial governments directly at http://canada.gc.ca/othergov/prov_e.html.

• You can also access provincial and territorial government sites and all provincial and territorial welfare departments through the "Canadian Social Research Links" website at http://members.home.net/gilseg/index.htm.

For details on provincial and territorial government information on child support guidelines and programs, you can call the phone number for your province or territory listed on the following page.

Provincial/Territorial Government Phone Numbers

Alberta — for toll-free access	1-310-0000
Calgary	(403) 297-6600
Edmonton	(403) 415-0404
British Columbia	888-216-2211
Vancouver	(604) 660-2192
Manitoba	877-943-2631
New Brunswick	888-236-2444
Newfoundland	(709) 729-1831
Nova Scotia	800-665-9779
Halifax	(902) 455-3135
Northwest Territories	888-298-7880
Yellowknife	(867) 873-7044
Ontario	800-980-4962
Prince Edward Island	800-240-9798
Quebec	
Communication Québec	800-363-1363
Ministère de la Justice	
du Québec	(418) 643-5140
Saskatchewan	888-218-2822
Yukon	800-661-0408
Whitehorse	(403) 667-5437

Provincial/Territorial Non-Governmental Services

In addition to provincial and territorial government services, some provincial/territorial level voluntary organizations provide services and resources for families. A limited number of these organizations in your province or territory is listed in the Public Health Agency of Canada's Mental Health Promotion Unit website (see box on page 63).

61

Government of Canada and National Voluntary Organizations: They're Closer Than You Think

Although federal government departments may seem distant, they provide resources and information available to all Canadians. As with provincial and territorial government offices and services, refer to the Blue Pages of the phone book or the Internet.

Government of Canada

- For phone numbers of federal departments or services, refer to the government Blue Pages under "Government of Canada."

The primary Internet site for the Government of Canada is http://canada.gc.ca/ or you can contact federal departments that have Internet facilities at http://canada.gc.ca/depts/major/depind_e.html. Another website for all Canadian government home pages and federal government sites is http://members.home.net/gilseg/index.htm.

Public Health Agency of Canada

The Public Health Agency of Canada publication *Guide to Federal Programs and Services for Children and Youth* provides information on existing federal programs and services for parents, families, professionals and organizations that work with children. Copies may be obtained by contacting:

    Division of Childhood and Adolescence
    Centre for Health Promotion
    Public Health Agency of Canada
    200 Eglantine Driveway
    Jeanne Mance Building
    Address Locator: 1909C2
    Tunney's Pasture
    Ottawa ON K1A 0K9
    Tel.: (613) 952-1220
    Fax: (613) 952-1556
    http://www.phac-aspc.gc.ca/dca-dea/main_e.html
    e-mail: DCA_public_inquiries@phac-aspc.gc.ca

The Public Health Agency of Canada's Mental Health Promotion Unit Website

http://www.mentalhealthpromotion.com

The Mental Health Promotion Unit website of the Public Health Agency of Canada highlights programs and resources related to the topic of mental health promotion. Mental health promotion is built on the foundation of fostering personal resilience through empowering all individuals to strengthen their coping skills, self-esteem and ability to effectively utilize the resources offered by a supportive community.

This website includes a section called *Because Life Goes On...* that contains information and resources which complement and expand on the information included in this booklet.

Department of Justice Canada

The Federal Child Support Guidelines set the basic amount of child support that a paying parent should pay. This amount depends on where the parents live, the number of children, and the paying parent's income. One purpose of the Guidelines is to reduce conflict and the need for lengthy negotiations regarding the amount of child support. In this way, parents can determine, with more certainty, the amount of child support a court would order.

For more information about the Federal Child Support Guidelines, or to order free child support publications, please call the Department of Justice Canada, toll free, at 1-888-373-2222. Publications include a pamphlet entitled *Child Support Guidelines: Kids Come First*; a 28-page booklet entitled *Federal Child Support Guidelines: A Guide to the New Approach*; a *Workbook for Parents*; and the simplified child support tables for the particular province or territory. Or, you may order these publications by writing to: Publications, Child Support Team, Department of Justice Canada, 284 Wellington Street, Ottawa ON K1A 0H8.

Please make sure you specify where each parent lives, and how many children from this relationship are involved, so that the federal government can send you the relevant tables. Many of the publications are also on the Department of Justice Canada's Internet site under Child Support at http://canada.justice.gc.ca.

Quebec residents can obtain a publication from the *Ministère de la Justice du Québec* (Department of Justice) on the Quebec model for the determination of child support payments, at http://www.justice.gouv.qc.ca/anglais/index-a.htm. Another brochure entitled *Médiation, fixation, défiscalisation (des pensions alimentaires) : comprendre les changements*, is available for a small fee from the *Ministère du Revenu du Québec*. Call 1-800-267-6299.

National Voluntary Organizations

A number of non-government organizations across Canada take an active interest in enhancing the well-being of children and families. Some give hands-on help directly to family members while others carry out research and public education programs that benefit families. A few of these organizations, along with a description of their programs, resources and/or services, are listed in the Public Health Agency of Canada's Mental Health Promotion Unit website (see box on page 63).

Other National and International Efforts

Refer to the Public Health Agency of Canada's Mental Health Promotion Unit website (see box on page 63) for more information on the following national and international efforts to improve the well-being of children, youth and families:
• The Special Joint Committee on Child Custody and Access
• The United Nations Convention on the Rights of the Child.

What Do I Do When…?

… I Need to Find Quality Child Care in My Community

• Ask friends, family members and neighbours if they can recommend a child care program in your area.

- Look in the government Blue Pages for provincial and municipal "child care information and referral agencies" or "child care benefits."
- Some larger cities have community-wide information and referral agencies. Contact the United Way or other community organizations. Ask them whether this service exists in your area.
- The Canadian Child Care Federation is a national non-profit, service-based organization committed to improving the quality of child care services in Canada. If you need information on child care or would like a referral, you can contact them at:

> Canadian Child Care Federation
> 383 Parkdale Avenue, Suite 201
> Ottawa ON K1Y 4R4
> Tel.: (613) 729-5289 or toll-free at 1-800-858-1412
> Fax: (613) 729-3159
> Email: cccf@sympatico.ca
> http://www.cfc-efc.ca/cccf ("Child and Family Canada" website)

The Child and Family Canada website contains a series of resource sheets on child care issues that you can obtain on-line, such as:
- *What is Quality Child Care?*
- *How do You Find Quality Care?*
- *Being an Effective Child Care Parent*
- *The Child Care Partnership: Managing and Monitoring Your Child Care*
- *Quality Child Care: A Parent's Role*

The complete list of resource sheets is available on the website.

... I Have Financial Needs

If you do not have an income (for example, you've left your partner), you can apply for social assistance. Your needs will be determined based on documentation you will be asked to supply. The assistance may pay for food, fuel, medical insurance, education allowance, daycare and clothing. In an emergency, social assistance can give you money immediately, and you don't need to wait to apply until you're completely out of money.

A child and family service organization will be able to give you information on where and how to get financial assistance. Or refer to the government Blue Pages under provincial and municipal government for "Social Assistance."

The website "Canadian Social Research Links" (http://members. home.net/gilseg/index.htm) has a list of all provincial and territorial government departments responsible for social assistance.

... I Want to Learn More About Family Mediation Services

Lawyers are now required by law to tell you about various ways a separating couple can negotiate to reach an agreement. Family mediation has become recognized as a way to solve family problems outside the court system. Before obtaining the services of a mediator, find out about her or his training and experience in mediating your type of case, fees charged, references, and whether the mediator has been certified by Family Mediation Canada. Some lawyers offer mediation on parenting and financial issues on a fee-for-service basis; they may be listed in the Yellow Pages.

The family mediation process varies between provinces and territories. For example:

- In Quebec since 1997, separating couples with dependent children may receive services of a mediator free of charge. Separating couples with dependent children may not be heard by the court without first attending a session about the mediation process (unless exempted by a mediator).
- In Manitoba, mediation on parenting issues is available at no cost through trained mediators at Family Conciliation, a provincial government service (1-800-282-8069 ext. 7236). Parents are required to attend a free supportive information seminar, "For the Sake of the Children." Once parents complete the program and agree to proceed with mediation, Family Conciliation will assign a mediator, at no cost.

Family Mediation Canada (FMC) is a non-profit association providing information and a referral service, and offers support and training for its membership of 1000 mediators across Canada. FMC also offers information resources such as:

- *Family Mediation: Consumer's Guide*
- *Facing Divorce: Look Into Mediation*
- *Making Mediation Referrals for Separating or Divorcing Couples*
- *Positive Parenting*

FMC has a comprehensive video-lending library appropriate for private study. It has also published a *Canadian Inventory of Parent Education Programs During Separation and Divorce,* which describes over 130 programs. An order form is available on FMC's website.

For more information on family mediation, a listing of family mediators in your community, and to order materials, contact:

> Family Mediation Canada
> 528 Victoria Street North
> Kitchener ON N2H 5G1
> Tel.: (519) 585-3118
> Fax: (519) 585-3121
> Email: fmc@fmc.ca
> http://www.fmc.ca

For specific information pertaining to family mediation and who to contact in your province or territory, refer to the Public Health Agency of Canada's Mental Health Promotion Unit website (see box on page 63).

... I Need Legal Information and Services

Most of the provinces and territories have the following organizations or services to help you with the legal aspects of separation and divorce. To find their addresses and phone numbers, refer to the Yellow Pages under "lawyers" or "legal services," or in the provincial and territorial government Blue Pages look under the headings "Justice" or "Attorney General."

Arbitration is another way, like mediation, of dealing with a dispute out of court. An arbitrator is an independent person, often a lawyer jointly chosen by the parties involved who, can hear and decide their dispute. The arbitration process is similar to a court hearing but simpler and less formal.

Public Legal Education and Information Organizations (PLEIs), which operate in each province and territory throughout Canada, provide free legal information. These organizations also distribute free pamphlets for the general public on family law, separation and divorce, and other legal topics.

Access to Justice Network (http://www.acjnet.org/) is an electronic community that brings together people, information and educational resources on Canadian justice and legal issues. It includes law and justice resource materials, as well as directories on Canadian public legal education organizations, Canadian law firms, lawyers, judges and government departments. ACJNet is the only nationwide service dedicated to making law and justice resources available to all Canadians in both official languages.

Legal Aid Services — Each province and territory has Legal Aid Services, available to those who meet their financial eligibility requirements. If you cannot afford a lawyer, you may qualify for these services.

Lawyer Referral Services — In many provinces you can call the "lawyer referral service" toll- free, for the names of three lawyers in your area who might best help you with your case. Some province referal services charge a nominal fee of approximately $25.00 for the initial consultation service, while others are free of charge. Lawyers are also listed in the Yellow Pages and some indicate that they specialize in family law.

Legal Information Phone Service is a free program in some provinces that offers general legal information on a wide variety of topics. Using a touch-tone phone, callers can listen to brief tape-recorded messages in everyday language.

The **Provincial/Territorial Bar Association or Law Society** may provide services such as lawyer referrals and free legal information over the telephone. They can also put you in touch with the Public Legal Education and Information office and Legal Aid Office in your province or territory.

Community Legal Clinics — Some areas may have local community legal clinics. A clinic can advise you about your rights or refer you to other sources of help.

... My Family Is Experiencing Violence

Ask for assistance. Friends, family members or your family doctor may be able to offer support and direct you to appropriate resources. Or refer to the inside cover or first few pages of the telephone book for numbers to call:

- "9-1-1" for emergency situations (in places where this service exists)
- Police, fire department or ambulance service
- The local child welfare agency (for concerns regarding child abuse)
- Distress centres (emergency help lines in your community)
- Rape Crisis Centre (sexual assault)
- Sexual assault victims
- Sexual assault treatment program
- Assault victims
- Shelter for abused women
- Kids Help Phone (1-800-668-6868) free anywhere in Canada.

The Yellow Pages of the phone book also lists community organizations that can help. Look under a heading such as "child welfare agency," "social service agency," "mental health centre," "legal clinic" and other community service organizations that provide counselling and support to children and families.

The government Blue Pages list city and provincial services and agencies. Because the names for these services differ from place to place, look for headings such as "child and family services," "children's services," "child abuse prevention," "family violence" or "community and social services."

For information about violence within the family and new resources being used to address it, you can contact The National Clearinghouse on Family Violence (NCFV). The NCFV is a national resource centre for all Canadians seeking information about and solutions to violence within the family. All clearinghouse services and publications are provided free of charge throughout Canada in both official languages.

In addition to the resources provided by the NCFV, the Clearinghouse recommends two additional resources for parents:

- *Fresh Start/Nouveau Départ* available through the YWCA of Canada. This booklet can be ordered by calling (416) 962-8881.
- *Leaving an Abusive Relationship: Help for You and Your Children* available through the BC Council for the Family. This pamphlet can be ordered by calling 1-800-663-5638.

For further information on family violence, contact:

National Clearinghouse on Family Violence
Family Violence Prevention Unit
Public Health Agency of Canada
200 Eglantine Driveway
Jeanne Mance Building, 9th floor
Address Locator: 1909D
Tunney's Pasture
Ottawa ON K1A 0K9
1-800-267-1291 or (613) 957-2938
Fax: (613) 941-8930
TTY: 1-800-561-5643 or (613) 952-6396
http://www.phac-aspc.gc.ca/nc-cn
e-mail: ncfv-cnivf@phac-aspc.gc.ca

Did you know that...?

VIOLET: Law and Abused Women (http://violetnet.org/) is an Internet site where you can find legal information that you may need if you are experiencing violence in an intimate relationship. This website has information on custody and divorce, and provides useful linkages to other relevant websites. There is also information on where to find a safe place or where to find assistance.

... I Would Like to Find Out About Support (Self-Help) Groups in My Community

Self-help groups are non-profit organizations that provide support and information for individuals living with a variety of physical and mental health problems and stressful life situations. Many self-help groups operate in communities across Canada. For example, there may be support groups for separated and divorced parents, single parents, or parents dealing with substance abuse or physical abuse. Some of these support groups may be listed in the telephone book, but many are not.

Self-help clearinghouses exist across Canada. Their purpose is to provide information about the variety of self-help groups that meet in their city or province, and how to locate them. Some of them publish a directory. The Self-Help Resource Centre of Greater Toronto has a website (http://www.selfhelp.on.ca) with useful information on self-help centres, links and resources. The Canadian Council on Social Development also has a publication available entitled *The Self-Help Way* that examines numerous facets of self-help/mutual aid. You can order this book and others on self-help by contacting CCSD at (613) 236-8977 or email them at: council@ccsd.ca.

Refer to the Public Health Agency of Canada's Mental Health Promotion Unit website (see box on page 63) for a list of some self-help clearinghouses located across Canada.

... We're Considering Marital Reconciliation

If couples are interested in pursuing marital reconciliation, they can seek guidance from self-help groups, trained therapists, mediators or health professionals. There are many websites on the Internet that contain resources, seminars and other services for couples in distress who wish to improve their marriage.

The Canadian Council on Social Development has a series of resources on marriage and relationship issues. A list of publications is available on their website: http://www.ccsd.ca/ or call (613) 236-8977.

Books and Videos for Parents, Children and Youth

This section lists a sampling of available reading, audio-visual and Internet material for families going through separation and divorce. Mental health professionals, social workers, mediators and other professionals may be useful in helping you choose the resources that best suit your needs. Specialized book stores may also be able to help. Ask them which resources they would recommend.

Books for Parents

Parenting after Separation and Divorce

BIENENFELD, FLORENCE. 1995 (reprint). *Helping Your Child Through Your Divorce*. Alameda, Calif.: Hunter House, Inc.

COLOROSO, BARBARA. 1995. *Kids Are Worth It! Giving Your Child the Gift of Inner Discipline*. Toronto: Somerville House Publishing.

KALTER, NEIL. 1991 (Ballanti edition). *Growing Up with Divorce: Helping Your Child Avoid Immediate and Later Emotional Problems*. New York: The Free Press.

NEUMAN, GARY M. and ROMANOWSKI, PATRICIA. 1999. *Helping Your Kids Cope with Divorce: The Sandcastles Way.* New York: Random House.

SCHNEIDER, MEG and ZUKERBERG, JOAN. 1996. *Difficult Questions Kids Ask, and are too Afraid to Ask, About Divorce.* New York: Fireside.

WALLERSTEIN, JUDITH and KELLY, JOAN. 1996 (reprint). *Surviving the Breakup: How Children and Parents Cope With Divorce.* New York: Basic Books Inc.

WOLF, ANTHONY. 1998. *"Why Did You Get a Divorce and WHEN Can I Get a Hamster": A Guide to Parenting through Divorce.* New York: Noonday Press.

Conflict Resolution

FISHER, ROGER and URY, WILLIAM. 1991 (2nd edition). *Getting to Yes: Negotiating Agreement Without Giving In.* New York: Penguin Books.

GOLD, LOIS. 1996 (reprint). *Between Love and Hate: A Guide to Civilized Divorce.* New York: Plenum Press.

Co-Parenting

BERNSTEIN, ROBERT and WORTH, RICHARD. 1996. *Divorced Dad's Handbook, 100 Questions and Answers.* Tempe, Ariz.: Blue Bird Publications.

BLAU, MELINDA. 1995. *Families Apart: Ten Keys to Successful Co-Parenting.* New York: Perigree.

RICCI, ISOLINA. 1997 (revised edition). *Mom's House, Dad's House: A Complete Guide for Parents who are Separated, Divorced or Remarried.* New York: Fireside.

THOMAS, SHIRLEY. 1995. *Parents are Forever, A Step-by-Step Guide to Becoming Successful Coparents after Divorce.* Longmont, Colo.: Springboard Publications.

TILLEY, DWIGHT. 1994. *Questions from Dad: A Very Cool Way to Communicate with Kids.* Boston: Charles Tuttle Company, Inc.

Step-Parenting

GREENE MULFORD, PHILIPPA. 1996. *Keys to Successful Step-Mothering*. Hauppauge, N.Y.: Barron's Educational Series, Inc.

KELLEY, PATRICIA. 1995. *Developing Healthy Stepfamilies, Twenty Families Tell Their Stories*. New York: The Harrington Park Press.

MARSHALL, PETER. 1993. *Cinderella Revisited, How to Survive a Step Family Without a Fairy Godmother*. Vancouver: Whitecap Books.

WALLERSTEIN, JUDITH and BLAKESLEE, SANDRA. 1996 (revised edition). *Second Chances: Men, Women, and Children a Decade After Divorce*. New York: Ticknor & Fields.

Books for Children and Youth

Preschoolers and Elementary

BROWN, LAURENCE and BROWN, MARC. 1988 (reprint). *Dinosaur's Divorce: A Guide for Changing Families*. New York: Little Brown. (Ages 4–8).

CASELEY, JUDITH. 1995. *Priscilla Twice*. New York: Greenwillow Books. (Ages 4–8).

FIELD, MARY. 1994. *My Life Turned Upside Down, but I Turned It Rightside Up*. King of Prussia, Pa.: Center for Applied Psychology. (Ages 7–11).

GROLLMAN, EARL A. 1989. *Talking About Divorce and Separation: A Dialogue Between Parent and Child*. New York: Beacon Press. (Ages 6–8).

JENNESS, AYLETTE. 1990. *Families: A Celebration of Diversity, Commitment, and Love*. Boston: Houghton Mifflin Company. (Ages 7+)

STERN, ZOE and STERN, EVAN. 1998. *Divorce is Not the End of the World: Zoe's and Evan's Coping Guide for Kids*. Berkeley, Calif.: Ten Speed Press.

Teenagers

HIPP, EARL. 1995. *Help for the Hard Times: Getting Through the Loss.* Center City, Minn.: Hazelden.

KIMBALL, GAYLE. 1994. *How to Survive Your Parents' Divorce: Kids' Advice to Kids.* Chico, Calif.: Equality Press.

Videos for Parents, Children and Youth

A good place to start looking for videos is your public library. Your public library has a catalogue of English and French videos produced by the National Film Board of Canada (NFB).

The NFB is a public agency that produces and distributes films and other audio-visual works that reflect Canada to Canadians and the rest of the world. They have several broad subjects and genre categories, including sub-categories that look at divorce and separation, family violence, problems in the family, violence against women, single mothers, child rearing and development. Visit their website at http://www.nfb.ca/. In particular, we suggest:

"One Divided by Two: Kids and Divorce" is a 24-minute video produced by the NFB (1998) which focuses on 13 young people (ages 8–18) whose parents have divorced. The animated video describes the heightened feelings, dreams, hopes and memories triggered by divorcing parents, and uncovers the lyricism and humour of painful events. For ages 10 and up. You can call the NFB at 1-800-267-7710 to order the video ($39.95, order number: C9197).

The National Clearinghouse on Family Violence (NCFV) has an up-to-date catalogue, *Preventing Family Violence*, of Canadian videos on family violence for the general public and for professionals working in the field. The videos have been carefully reviewed by the professional staff at the NCFV to ensure that they are sensitive, useful, modern and relevant. Contact them at 1-800-267-1291. Their website is http://www.phac-aspc.gc.ca/nc-cn.

The Ministry of the Attorney General of Ontario has recently produced a video entitled "Separate Ways." (1998). It offers insights from those who have gone through separation and divorce and from professionals who have assisted them. It also discusses dealing with emotions, the impact on children, and mediation. This video is available through local family courts and libraries in Ontario. (Available in English, French, Mandarin, Cantonese, Portuguese, Vietnamese, Polish, Somali, Spanish, Sign Language, open captioning French, open captioning English).

"Kids Talk About Divorce" is a video intended for therapeutic/educational use. Children aged 6–14 describe their struggles and successes in coping with divorce. Created by Families in Transition (Family Service Association of Toronto), the video and companion guide are available for $100. Contact Families in Transition at: 2 Carlton Street, Suite 917, Toronto, Ontario M5B 1JS, or fax 416-586-0031, email fit@fsatoronto.com

Notes

....
....
....
....
....
....
....
....
....
....
....
....
....
....
....
....
....
....
....
....
....

Notes

....

....

....

....

....

....

....

....

....

....

....

....

....

....

....

....

....

....

....

Notes

....
....
....
....
....
....
....
....
....
....
....
....
....
....
....
....
....
....
....
....

Notes

....

....

....

....

....

....

....

....

....

....

....

....

....

....

....

....

....

....

....

....

ORDER FORM

Please send:

———— English copy(ies) *Because Life Goes On — Helping Children and Youth Live with Separation and Divorce* (CAT. H39-293/1994E)

———— French copy(ies) *Parce que la vie continue — Aider les enfants et les adolescents à vivre la séparation et le divorce* (CAT. H39-293/1994F)

_____
NAME   ORGANIZATION

_____
ADDRESS

_____
CITY   PROVINCE   POSTAL CODE

_____
TELEPHONE   FAX

How did you find the overall quality and usefulness of the information contained in this booklet?

☐ Poor   ☐ Good   ☐ Very good

Which section of the booklet did you find…

Most helpful: _____ Least helpful: _____

Would you recommend this booklet to someone you know who is going through separation or divorce?

☐ Yes   ☐ No   Please explain: _____

Do you have any comments or suggestions on how this booklet could be improved?

_____

_____

_____

Fax your order to: (613) 941-5366

Or mail to: Publications
                     Public Health Agency of Canada
                     Postal locator 0913A
                     Ottawa, Ontario
                     K1A 0K9
                     Telephone: (613) 957-2991

This publication is also available on the Internet at the following address: www.mentalhealthpromotion.com